PRAISE AND WORSHIP
FOR CLASSICAL PIANO

15 BEAUTIFUL ARRANGEMENTS BY PHILLIP KEVEREN

T0083357

— PIANO LEVEL —
INTERMEDIATE

ISBN 978-1-70515-557-8

Visit Hal Leonard Online at
www.halleonard.com

Visit Phillip at
www.phillipkeveren.com

Contact us:
Hal Leonard
7777 West Bluemound Road
Milwaukee, WI 53213
Email: info@halleonard.com

In Europe, contact:
Hal Leonard Europe Limited
42 Wigmore Street
Marylebone, London, W1U 2RN
Email: info@halleonardeurope.com

In Australia, contact:
Hal Leonard Australia Pty. Ltd.
4 Lentara Court
Cheltenham, Victoria, 3192 Australia
Email: info@halleonard.com.au

PREFACE

Using classical compositional devices, these praise and worship songs have been developed into character pieces for piano solo. The term "classical" gets tossed about widely in the world of music. In this application, my guiding goal is to fashion an arrangement that feels more like a composition created expressly for the piano.

Whether played in a worship service or recital, I hope these settings will enrich your enjoyment of music in general, and the pleasure of pursuing keyboard artistry in particular.

Phillip Keveren

BIOGRAPHY

Phillip Keveren, a multi-talented keyboard artist and composer, has composed original works in a variety of genres from piano solo to symphonic orchestra. He gives frequent concerts and workshops for teachers and their students in the United States, Canada, Europe, and Asia. Mr. Keveren holds a B.M. in composition from California State University Northridge and a M.M. in composition from the University of Southern California.

CONTENTS

ANCIENT WORDS

Words and Music by LYNN DeSHAZO
Arranged by Phillip Keveren

AS THE DEER

Words and Music by MARTIN NYSTROM
Arranged by Phillip Keveren

BUILD YOUR KINGDOM HERE

Words and Music by REND COLLECTIVE
Arranged by Phillip Keveren

With joyful energy ♩ = 138

HERE I AM TO WORSHIP
(Light of the World)

Words and Music by TIM HUGHES
Arranged by Phillip Keveren

HE IS EXALTED

Words and Music by TWILA PARIS
Arranged by Phillip Keveren

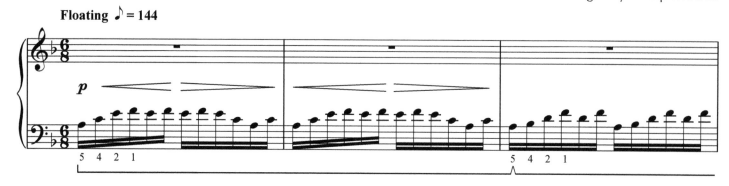

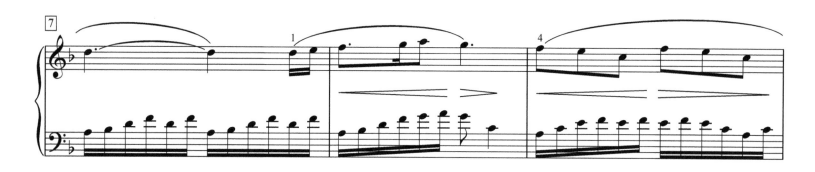

LIVING HOPE

Words and Music by PHIL WICKHAM
and BRIAN JOHNSON
Arranged by Phillip Keveren

MAJESTY

Words and Music by JACK HAYFORD
Arranged by Phillip Keveren

LORD, I LIFT YOUR NAME ON HIGH

Words and Music by RICK FOUNDS
Arranged by Phillip Keveren

O CHURCH ARISE

Words and Music by KEITH GETTY
and STUART TOWNEND
Arranged by Phillip Keveren

OUR GOD

Words and Music by JONAS MYRIN,
JESSE REEVES, CHRIS TOMLIN
and MATT REDMAN
Arranged by Phillip Keveren

Boldly ♩ = 108

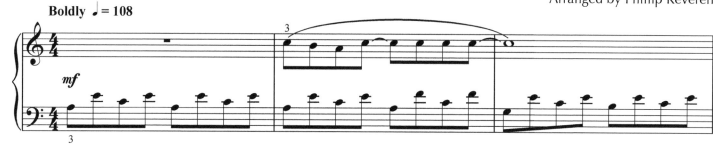

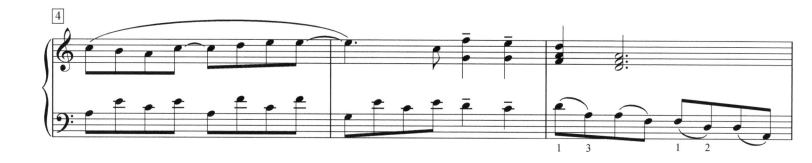

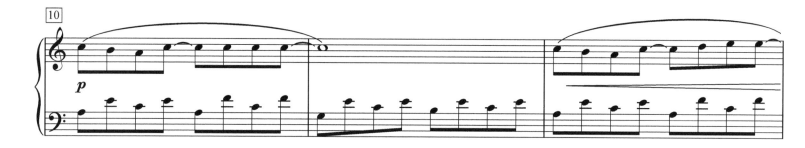

SPEAK O LORD

Words and Music by STUART TOWNEND
and KEITH GETTY
Arranged by Phillip Keveren

REVELATION SONG

Words and Music by JENNIE LEE RIDDLE
Arranged by Phillip Keveren

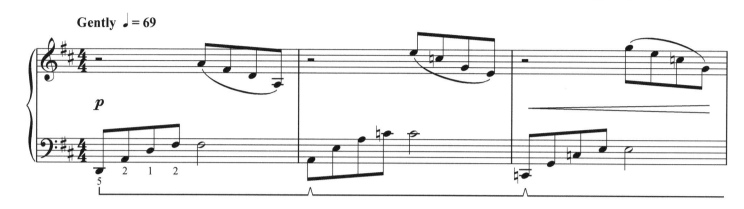

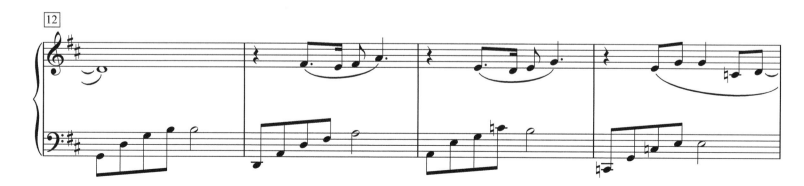

molto rit.

THERE IS A REDEEMER

Words and Music by MELODY GREEN
Arranged by Phillip Keveren

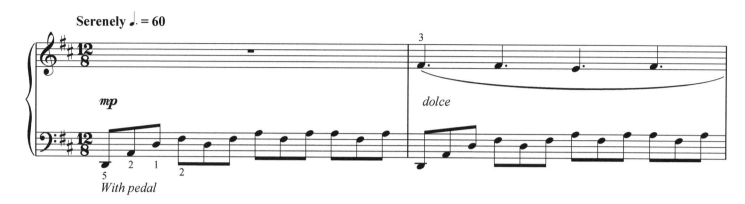

2

YET NOT I BUT THROUGH CHRIST IN ME

Words and Music by MICHAEL FARREN,
JONNY ROBINSON and RICH THOMPSON
Arranged by Phillip Keveren

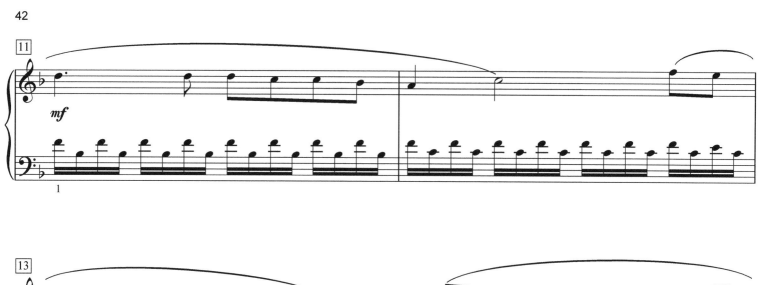

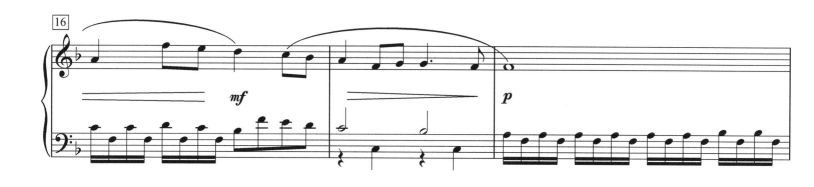

YOUR NAME

Words and Music by PAUL BALOCHE
and GLENN PACKIAM
Arranged by Phillip Keveren

THE PHILLIP KEVEREN SERIES

PIANO SOLO

00156644	ABBA for Classical Piano	$15.99
00311024	Above All	$12.99
00311348	Americana	$12.99
00198473	Bach Meets Jazz	$14.99
00313594	Bacharach and David	$15.99
00306412	The Beatles	$17.99
00312189	The Beatles for Classical Piano	$16.99
00275876	The Beatles – Recital Suites	$19.99
00312546	Best Piano Solos	$15.99
00156601	Blessings	$12.99
00198656	Blues Classics	$12.99
00284359	Broadway Songs with a Classical Flair	$14.99
00310669	Broadway's Best	$14.99
00312106	Canzone Italiana	$12.99
00280848	Carpenters	$16.99
00310629	A Celtic Christmas	$12.99
00310549	The Celtic Collection	$12.95
00280571	Celtic Songs with a Classical Flair	$12.99
00263362	Charlie Brown Favorites	$14.99
00312190	Christmas at the Movies	$14.99
00294754	Christmas Carols with a Classical Flair	$12.99
00311414	Christmas Medleys	$14.99
00236669	Christmas Praise Hymns	$12.99
00233788	Christmas Songs for Classical Piano	$12.99
00311769	Christmas Worship Medleys	$14.99
00310607	Cinema Classics	$15.99
00301857	Circles	$10.99
00311101	Classic Wedding Songs	$10.95
00311292	Classical Folk	$10.95
00311083	Classical Jazz	$12.95
00137779	Coldplay for Classical Piano	$16.99
00311103	Contemporary Wedding Songs	$12.99
00348788	Country Songs with a Classical Flair	$14.99
00249097	Disney Recital Suites	$17.99
00311754	Disney Songs for Classical Piano	$17.99
00241379	Disney Songs for Ragtime Piano	$17.99
00311881	Favorite Wedding Songs	$14.99
00315974	Fiddlin' at the Piano	$12.99
00311811	The Film Score Collection	$15.99
00269408	Folksongs with a Classical Flair	$12.99
00144353	The Gershwin Collection	$14.99
00233789	Golden Scores	$14.99
00144351	Gospel Greats	$12.99
00183566	The Great American Songbook	$12.99
00312084	The Great Melodies	$12.99
00311157	Great Standards	$12.95
00171621	A Grown-Up Christmas List	$12.99
00311071	The Hymn Collection	$12.99
00311349	Hymn Medleys	$12.99
00280705	Hymns in a Celtic Style	$12.99
00269407	Hymns with a Classical Flair	$12.99
00311249	Hymns with a Touch of Jazz	$12.99
00310905	I Could Sing of Your Love Forever	$12.95
00310762	Jingle Jazz	$14.99
00175310	Billy Joel for Classical Piano	$16.99
00126449	Elton John for Classical Piano	$16.99
00310839	Let Freedom Ring!	$12.99
00238988	Andrew Lloyd Webber Piano Songbook	$14.99
00313227	Andrew Lloyd Webber Solos	$15.99
00313523	Mancini Magic	$16.99
00312113	More Disney Songs for Classical Piano	$16.99
00311295	Motown Hits	$14.99
00300640	Piano Calm	$12.99
00339131	Piano Calm: Christmas	$12.99
00346009	Piano Calm: Prayer	$14.99
00306870	Piazzolla Tangos	$16.99
00156645	Queen for Classical Piano	$15.99
00310755	Richard Rodgers Classics	$16.99
00289545	Scottish Songs	$12.99
00310609	Shout to the Lord!	$14.99
00119403	The Sound of Music	$14.99
00311978	The Spirituals Collection	$10.99
00210445	Star Wars	$16.99
00224738	Symphonic Hymns for Piano	$14.99
00279673	Tin Pan Alley	$12.99
00312112	Treasured Hymns for Classical Piano	$14.99
00144926	The Twelve Keys of Christmas	$12.99
00278486	The Who for Classical Piano	$16.99
00294036	Worship with a Touch of Jazz	$12.99
00311911	Yuletide Jazz	$17.99

EASY PIANO

00210401	Adele for Easy Classical Piano	$15.99
00310610	African-American Spirituals	$10.99
00218244	The Beatles for Easy Classical Piano	$14.99
00218387	Catchy Songs for Piano	$12.99
00310973	Celtic Dreams	$12.99
00233686	Christmas Carols for Easy Classical Piano	$12.99
00311126	Christmas Pops	$14.99
00311548	Classic Pop/Rock Hits	$14.99
00310769	A Classical Christmas	$10.95
00310975	Classical Movie Themes	$12.99
00144352	Disney Songs for Easy Classical Piano	$12.99
00311093	Early Rock 'n' Roll	$14.99
00311997	Easy Worship Medleys	$12.99
00289547	Duke Ellington	$14.99
00160297	Folksongs for Easy Classical Piano	$12.99

00110374	George Gershwin Classics	$12.99
00310805	Gospel Treasures	$12.99
00306821	Vince Guaraldi Collection	$19.99
00160294	Hymns for Easy Classical Piano	$12.99
00310798	Immortal Hymns	$12.99
00311294	Jazz Standards	$12.99
00310744	Love Songs	$12.99
00233740	The Most Beautiful Songs for Easy Classical Piano	$12.99
00220036	Pop Ballads	$14.99
00311406	Pop Gems of the 1950s	$12.95
00311407	Pop Gems of the 1960s	$12.95
00233739	Pop Standards for Easy Classical Piano	$12.99
00102887	A Ragtime Christmas	$12.99
00311293	Ragtime Classics	$10.95
00312028	Santa Swings	$12.99
00233688	Songs from Childhood for Easy Classical Piano	$12.99
00103258	Songs of Inspiration	$12.99
00310840	Sweet Land of Liberty	$12.99
00126450	10,000 Reasons	$14.99
00310712	Timeless Praise	$12.95
00311086	TV Themes	$12.99
00310717	21 Great Classics	$12.99
00160076	Waltzes & Polkas for Easy Classical Piano	$12.99
00145342	Weekly Worship	$16.99

BIG-NOTE PIANO

00310838	Children's Favorite Movie Songs	$12.99
00346000	Christmas Movie Magic	$12.99
00277368	Classical Favorites	$12.99
00310907	Contemporary Hits	$12.99
00277370	Disney Favorites	$14.99
00310888	Joy to the World	$12.99
00310908	The Nutcracker	$12.99
00277371	Star Wars	$16.99

BEGINNING PIANO SOLOS

00311202	Awesome God	$12.99
00310837	Christian Children's Favorites	$12.99
00311117	Christmas Traditions	$10.99
00311250	Easy Hymns	$12.99
00102710	Everlasting God	$10.99
00311403	Jazzy Tunes	$10.95
00310822	Kids' Favorites	$12.99
00338175	Silly Songs for Kids	$9.99

PIANO DUET

00126452	The Christmas Variations	$12.99
00311350	Classical Theme Duets	$10.99
00295099	Gospel Duets	$12.99
00311544	Hymn Duets	$14.99
00311203	Praise & Worship Duets	$12.99
00294755	Sacred Christmas Duets	$12.99
00119405	Star Wars	$14.99
00253545	Worship Songs for Two	$12.99

ALSO AVAILABLE

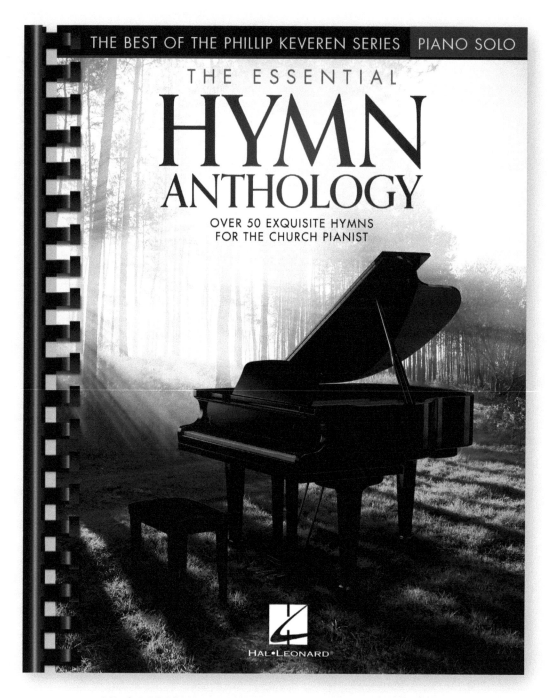

HL 364812 THE ESSENTIAL HYMN ANTHOLOGY
Church pianists will treasure this beautiful comb-bound
collection, the first in the Best of Phillip Keveren Series.